# Feathers

## or Love on the Wing

Elisavietta Ritchie

Megan Richard

***This book is dedicated to the author, Elisavietta Ritchie, whose poetry and spirit inspires the creation of this book and to Megan Richard, whose watercolors are poetry in and of themselves.***

*Book and chapbooks by the author:*

Tiger Upstairs on Connecticut Avenue (2013)
From the Artist's Deathbed (2012)
Cormorant Beyond the Compost (2011)
Real Toads (2008)
Awaiting Permission to Land (2006, CDs available upon request)
The Spirit of the Walrus (2005)
In Haste I Write You This Note: Stories & Half-Stories (2000)
The Arc of the Storm (1998)
Elegy for the Other Woman (1996)
Flying Time: Stories & Half-Stories (1992, 1996)
Wild Garlic: Journal of Maria X. (novella in verse, 1995)
A Wound-Up Cat & Other Bedtime Stories (1993)
The Problem with Eden (1985)
Raking the Snow (1982)
Moving to Larger Quarters (1977)
A Sheath of Dreams & Other Games (1976)
Tightening the Circle Over Eel Country (1974)
Timbot (novella in verse, 1970)

*Poetry anthologies edited:*

The Dolphin's Arc: Poems on Endangered Marine Species (1986)
Finding the Name (1983)
Here, Even the Blue Crabs Create (2009)

Feathers (or: Love on the Wing)

SUMMARY: a collection of poems by Elisavietta Ritchie, inspired by birds and certain humans, paired with collages of photographs of feathers and the watercolors of artist, Megan Richard.



Book design by Suzanne Shelden, Shelden Studios

ISBN 978-1-4675-5697-2

First Edition

Printed in the United States of America

# Table of Contents

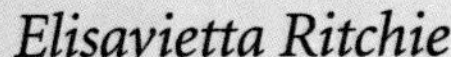

*Elisavietta Ritchie*

# "Without the Mind, Nothing Exists"

*for Taj, after a class of Tai Chi*

Yet the oversize hawk in the winter maple
perched there before we segued
toward our parking place
through rain which did not seem to exist
for we paid it no mind today
therefore did not get wet   only mist

Taj departed   the hawk stayed
we watched him watch us   then pivot his gaze
not to the mindless pigeons   first
toward the heedless young lady
who carted bags to the trash
bins behind the café

more intense the hawk checked for rats
which exist around black plastic bags
he knows his talons could easily slash
the moment we all disappeared   (you asked
with your mindless chatter   how fast
will somebody snap up our parking space)

I pay more mind to the hawk
he existed/exists   no fake
molded owl to scare pigeons away
he knew that he and the rats by the trash
and the girl behind the café
were real and worth the risk

of a dive   mindful of breakfast
he'll nab those genuine rats before he takes flight
and soar   while earthbound I
could not hold the pose of even a pigeon right
yet whether or not you or I exist
we must wing it anyway

## Snowy Owl, Ontario

I won't hear his wings,
only a flung *Twhit-twhoo.*
I wait all night on the roof deck,
crouch among barrels of earth.

The moon is so bright, colors show.

The barrels burst green beans
flecked maroon, yellow tomatoes,
purple basil, mint with lavender spires.
Surely he's not colorblind.

No mice here: the twilight tom,
patrols the deck, and disappears.
Would an owl snatch so big a cat?

Has he plummeted, fled?
The moon cycles, cycles the sky.

In the morning I note
claw marks on my arms.

## Yesterday's Owl

At twilight an owl in the crotch
of the dead sycamore across the marsh
did not fly away when you left.
He did not move. I watched.

At dawn only the black stump
of a broken branch, unnoticed at dusk,
stands out against snow and sky
bare of the usual vultures and jays.

Fluffing his silent wings, the phantom
owl continues to perch in a cleft
in my mind, a mind that so far fails
to acquire his vaunted wisdom.

Not weighing philosophical
concepts, moral conundrums—
more, the death of a target prey
versus his own survival,

for even a phantom hungers—
he listens for rustles, a squirrel,
mouse or vole, the complaints
of a shot duck from the bay.

Like death, the owl remains real.
He will continue to monitor the scene
from his sycamore, then vanish again,
like wisdom or you in our northern jungle.

# Ornithological Calculations

Enormous bald eagle preens on the locust tree
fallen over the cove—If I begged him to stay as
he is till I called you *Come see how the late sun*
*strikes the white on his breast, cap, tail feathers,*
*how these will burn orange with the setting sun—*
by the first word I spoke, he'd lift off, fly away.
Sometimes best to observe a new love in silence.

# John James Audubon: *Snowy Egret*

beside the canal

beached trains
gravel piles
rail yards
tangled tracks

tarps enshroud
peculiar shapes
muffle cacophonies
screeches of steel

harsh whistles
horns and clanks
scritches of beetles
squeals of rats

a different snowy egret
legs in slime
iridescent with oil
waits, and croaks

beyond the canal

## Geese

As if my first season of geese....
Fleets of previous autumns streamed
too high to break my sound barrier.

Then I chose warmer zones
for parakeets, hornbills, flamingos,
multi-colored affairs.

Somber only in feather,
a thousand geese skid over ice,
crowd in creases of cove between floes.

All honk at once
then all at once: quiet,
to mull over flight patterns and paths.

They dive for what fish and weed shoots
survive November.
Triangles of tails bob like buoys.

Again the dark is laced with their honking.
In shivers I stand on the dock,
ponder my own survival and flight...

Suddenly scared by something downriver
a thousand geese rise and roar past —
Invisible wings graze my face.

Strange angels...
The noise of their honking
almost erases the acrid silences

of old love in hot lands,
the querulous voice of the new
in these icy climes.

# In Flight

after a day of talking too much
one moment of solitude
not quite silence

parked for the night behind Rips Notel
en route to the Bay on Route 301
mountainous trucks a warring of noise

but nobody talking here      no TVs
lawn spring-green to harlequin woods
in the warm end-of-October sun

I perch on the Subaru tailgate
open a $1.25 carton of soup
sweet-and-sour to ease the throat

and consider every spoonful
(the fortune cookie message reads
*Lions on a Hunt Don't Roar)*

then a vee of Canada geese
flies querulous overhead until
all at once they still their wings

lose altitude over an unseen marsh
and twenty-four dark-gray angels
in silence vanish into the dusk

## Frontier Station

Birds ignore borders
overfly all maps' lines
lightly as song

We wait behind barriers and signs
burdened, documented
inventing our reasons

Awaiting our orders
ignoring all seasons
we keep our places

Birds keep their seasons
leave and return
whiten the barricades

Wings graze our grayed faces

## Swan Story

You kept hounding me, as
we lay on the feather bed,
now write something important,

so I went out to write
on the man who shot down whistling swans
while I stood alone on the cliff
overlooking the frozen cove,
my boots soaked with slush
and mittens too thin,

and how I'd shot him
(simpler to shoot down a man
than a startled bird)

but I was so quick
he'd no time to be startled,
he dropped in the snow on the beach
reddening like the swan,

and no one who has seen swans in flight
or floating over the waves
or parading on ice too thin for a man,
or heard all night in the inlets and bays
their *woo-ho woo-woo woo-ho*
or however the bird books try
in vain to describe their whistles and cries,

no one who knows swans would dispute
that mine was a crime of passion,
a gesture of self-preservation—
you, also, love swans, would lie
to provide me with alibis—

so I buried the gun in an old woodchuck hole
then, retracing my way through the snow,
dragged a branch over my tracks,
brought it home to add to the fire,
and sat down to write my story for you,

but you said, O where have you been
out there all this time
in the cold and it's already dark,

you are soaked and spoiling the rug,
come to bed with me quickly, get warm,

so I never got to my story at all,
but next week I will
if the swans have flown back to the cove.

# Trading in Essentials, November

"A torrent of shooting stars due tonight,
between two and four a.m., says Weather."
You close down your server for dinner.

Eleven p.m. bundled in coats, by flashlight
we dodge fallen trees to the dock.
All stars remain glued to their universe.

Most birds gone in November. "A bummer,"
you shiver. "Best get some rest, must first check
my stocks—" We give up the night to sleep.

Insomnia hits me at two. Jacket wrapped
against cold, I navigate the yard blind,
lie back on the dock, and study the sky.

How many around the earth wait years
for omens, signs, change (any way or kind),
birth, death, help in the dark, a star?

At last, through the Milky Way, one flash
seems to burn through space, disappear.
A heron croaks low, vanishes into black.

Nothing more. Frozen, I seek the warm bed.
Though awake until dawn, one shot meteor
and one bird are perfectly fine, and worth the night.

## Insomnia Cantatas

These interruptions, I have known:
midnight gunfire, burglars, hurricane,
a lover or the lack, tidal flood,

that sudden rush of blood
and, more frequent now, the pierce of pain—
my malformed bones.

*This* is just another broken night,
of late more rare
thanks to makeshift peace, and age, and locks,

though one nocturnal thief, a rusty fox,
steals indoors to filch the kitten's fare.
Simply: I did not write

all day—
no, many days when barren pages
heap like futile clouds or arctic snows,

and wasted brilliance flows—
snowflakes melting into rain—and I must hide my rage
as unused hours swirl down the drain, away

and gone—
Such nights I wake at four
or barely sleep at all.

Thank God this winter night I hear the calls
of tundra swans camped in the cove, unlock the door
to let in swan cantatas, hungry fox, lover, words, and not too soon, the dawn.

# Feathers (or: Love on the Wing)

The lovers sent feathers
each to the other
for years.

Could not send letters,
flowers
or rings.

Feathers from jays as bold
as their goals,
shimmering, indigo blue.

Crimson—from a cardinal which sang
the morning they sprang
upon an unfeathered bed.

Plumes in rainbows of hues,
tropics of passions
too exotic to last.

Brown-beige feathers from wrens
which flew twigs to their sills,
the windows too far apart.

Fluff plucked from the breasts
to soften impossible nests
where no eggs would lie.

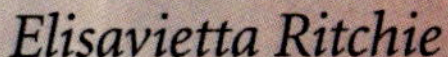


Wing quills of eagles mottled and barred
as their lives, one tail feather, white,
lost in flight.

Snowy feathers from tundra swans,
one from an antipodal ibis, black,
to tell how far each had fled.

Iridescent feathers of mourning doves
calling for desperate hours
through separate woods.

When the owl called, ebony crows
crowded into the field, bringing night
on their wings.

Aviaries of feathers lined
the insides of their graves,
bore them away.

Feathers continue to drift
on currents of wind, glide
toward both of the lovers.

Then, like butterflies, feathers land
on unfamiliar fingers,
their own outstretched hands.

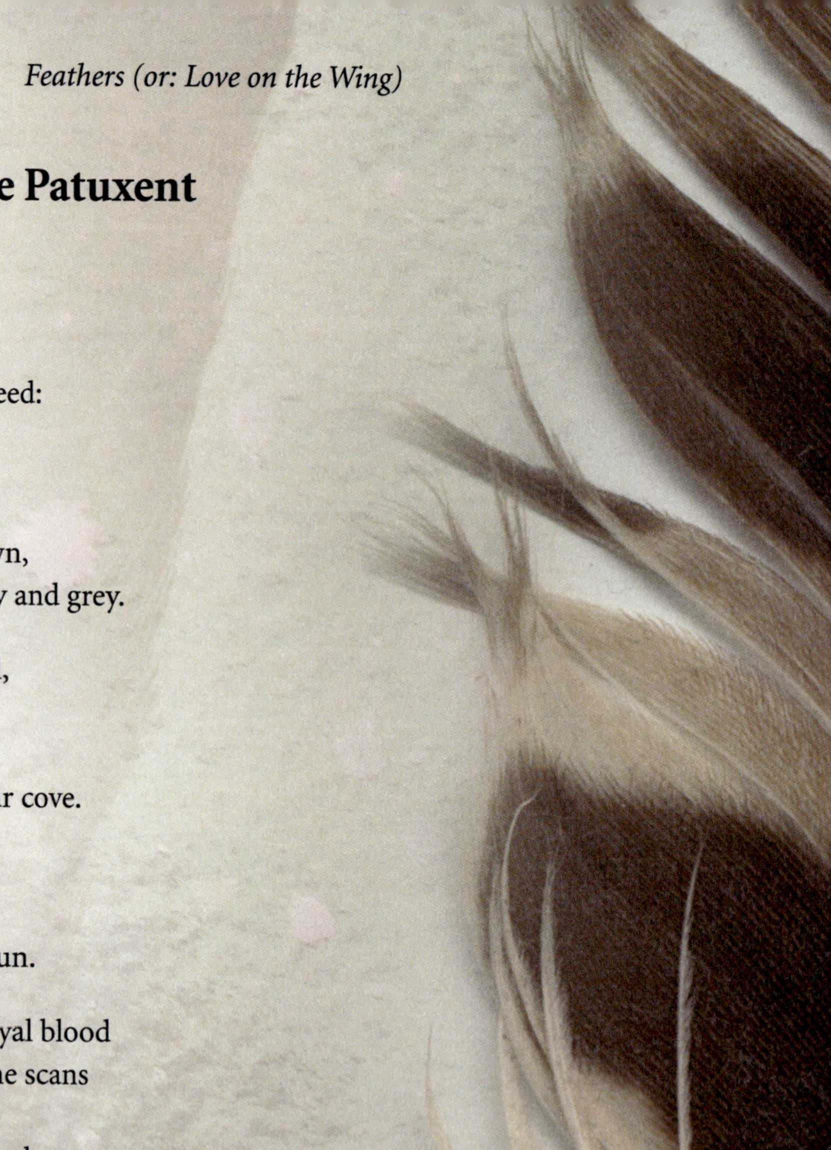

## Odette Plies the Patuxent

She's here to be fed.
Surely she's fine
pulling up seaweed
yet claims a different need:

she's abandoned. Nine
days ago I tossed bread
to a pair of swans, grown,
with four cygnets, fluffy and grey.

All the rest disappeared,
flown off and veered
south to the bay.
Now only one prods our cove.

She spies me here
and paddles over.
I hurry to find a stale bun.

A princess or nun of royal blood
banished, bewitched, she scans
the sky and prays
not for some common cob

but a wizard to wave his wand
over a neighboring bog
with a disconsolate princeling-swan,
change him to a full-blown king,
and transform her to a queen.

## Osprey

No fabled falcon
trained to wrists
of prince or feudal lord.

This rough bird builds
a scraggly nest of sticks
atop a piling, dead tree,

channel marker swirled
by tides and prey
to floods and hurricanes.

His cry is but a tenor peep
too feeble to spur fear
in fish or beast.

Yet when he soars,
rides the waves of sky,
his shadow knifes the sea,

when he plummets through
his talons spear their prize,
and he bears it home.

## Dinner Partners

Alone in the garden, twilight,
by a cove far from any town,
I'm eating an omelet: turkey
pastrami, onion, Swiss cheese.

Someone stalks up beside me.
Muscles tighten, fingers fist.

Turkey vulture two feet away!

They usually choose the far side
of the road to pick at their meal
but flee when disturbed. Always
on the job, covens patrol the sky,
hang out over a promising field.

Silent, this vulture strolls near
my splintery table, studies me,
stays. Immobile, I study him…

Plumage: glossy, slate-colored,
well-groomed as if for the visit.

Head solid gray: juvenile chick.
Shoved from his cluttered nest
in the tangled wood to fly solo?

What to teach me of solitude?

He rasps greetings or message,
his laryngitis worse than mine.

Is he lonely, or hungry? I fling
a fragment of omelet. He sniffs,
beaks it, flaps off over the cove.

Might he ever return? Too many
dying around me or gone, I need
soul-mates, familiars. Was this
a chance visitation, or an omen?

## Epilogue

Admire the vulture
ugly, ungainly while guarding
a stolen meal on the road

When on obsidian wings he soars
scans the land, clears the dead,
what a useful, elegant bird

Moonprints on the sea
will be absorbed
bones disintegrate

Feathers drifted to the sand
words scattered on the page of mind
may last

## Fledglings

En route to the jail
hesitating: is another rescue

possible, worth it or
should we leave things

and wings and him
alone,

on the parapet of the outside stairs
high above the wet parking lot

a starling, new, fuzz unkempt,
squawks and squawks —

I have vertigo too
so far to fall.

I understand the orphan condition
would carry him inside for crumbs

but already the motel-room lock
has clicked behind me —

and I'm already late for court —
for sure now I must go. —

## Presumptions

Who am I to try
to banish sparrows
from the feeder
just filled up
with fancy seeds
for fancier birds.

Right back anyway.
I step close enough
to scare them off
but discern their
markings: dusty,
discreet, elegant.

## In Search of Permanence

*"Today an artist must expect to write in water*
*and to cast in sand."* Cyril Connolly

I wrote a poem upon the beach,
marked it with a turquoise stone,
thought it quite safe, out of reach
of surf...

One
gull
dropped
down
alone
printed stanzas on my sand
in hieroglyphs I could not read.
Did he read mine?
Next
a
band
of peeping pipers came to feed
and scratch their verses, overlaid.

Then one tumbling racing wave

rushed in –
erased –
I tried to wade
to snatch our art, but could not save
one single verse or hieroglyph.

Next time I'll find a flat black pond,
row out in a narrow skiff.
When all is quiet, well beyond
my ripples, I will trace my rhymes
across those waters still and high.
Then wait and watch…Perhaps this time
my
words
will
mirror
in
the
sky.

## Visitations: Omens

Huge birds descend on the sand. Will they weave
a nest lined with down from their breasts,
leave an enormous egg, perhaps of gold?
Or an ungainly chick for me to raise?

Shrills, caws, clanks of beaks; cacophonous communiqués.
Feathered battalions measure me—for a feast?
Scimitar claws would bear me through thunderclouds
to consume on a distant branch or beach.

I scatter crumbs, seeds, whole loaves, then
the fish I unhook, anything to appease
such disturbing guests who do not tell me why
they have come, why they won't fly away.

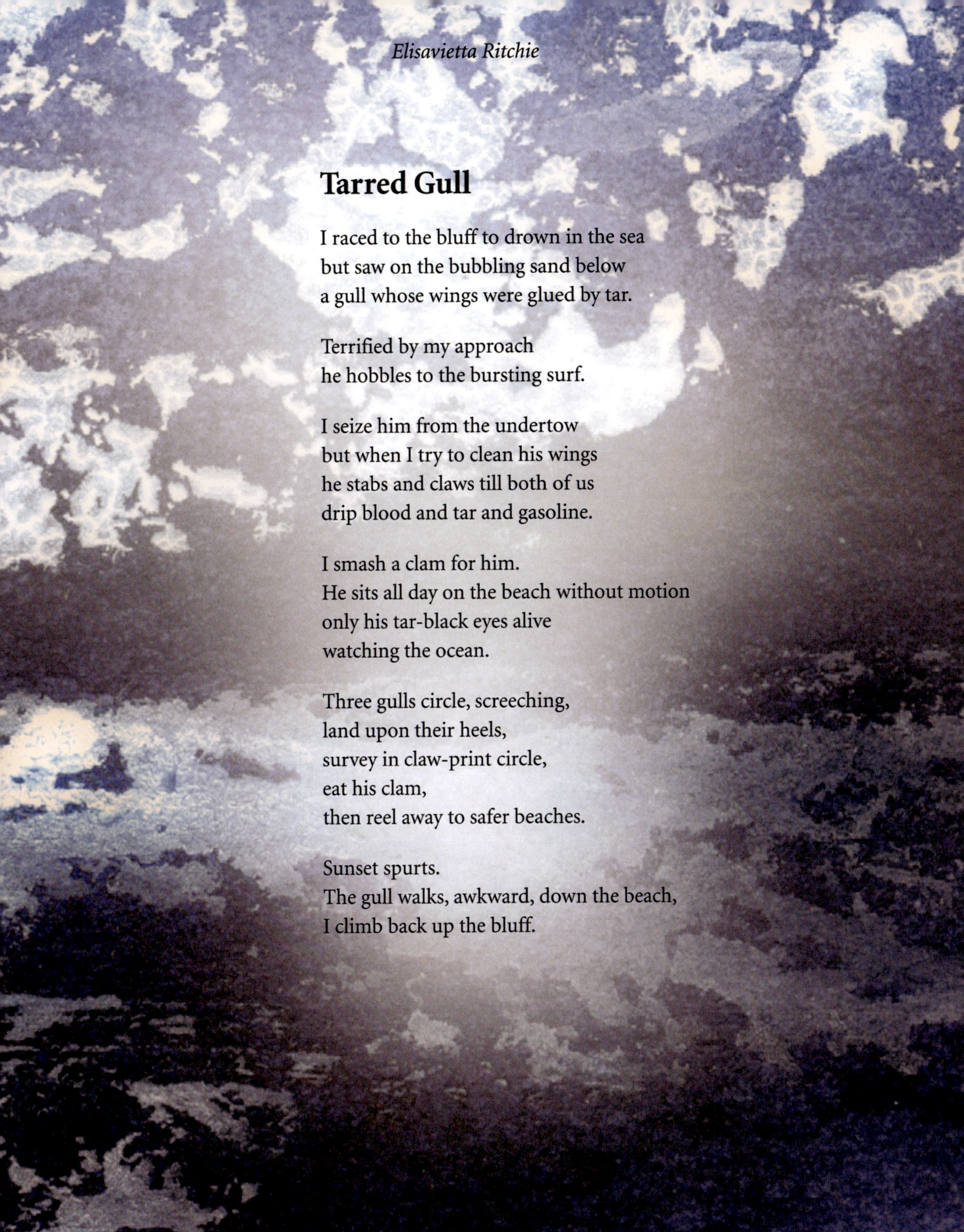

# Tarred Gull

I raced to the bluff to drown in the sea
but saw on the bubbling sand below
a gull whose wings were glued by tar.

Terrified by my approach
he hobbles to the bursting surf.

I seize him from the undertow
but when I try to clean his wings
he stabs and claws till both of us
drip blood and tar and gasoline.

I smash a clam for him.
He sits all day on the beach without motion
only his tar-black eyes alive
watching the ocean.

Three gulls circle, screeching,
land upon their heels,
survey in claw-print circle,
eat his clam,
then reel away to safer beaches.

Sunset spurts.
The gull walks, awkward, down the beach,
I climb back up the bluff.

## Dialogue with Mourning Dove

Notes of silk float through meadows dulled
by August drought… *April's* mating trills!

Forget it, bird, no would-be mate
returns unseasonal calls so late.

Summer's dust has dimmed last spring's
onyx hatpin eyes, iridescent head and wings.

Love-warbles now indecent, your bill
and coos *are* haunting still.

Fly home, repair your messy nest
not woven with a wren's finesse

but stuck one twig upon the next,
lost game of pick-up-sticks, a flimsy mess

and prey to hurricanes. No purpose to rebuild.
Low market for disheveled real estate. Unfulfilled,

you'll never soar like hawks or owls
to nab the hapless mole below,

or plummet osprey-style for fish or bait.
You're stuck with seeds, so face your fate.

Your departing whirr scarce agitates
the heavy air… Sudden echoes, desperate.

At dusk you reappear, re-paired—
doubled by a smoky troubadour!

So, on with coos, and on with love, although
you must remember how these matters go.

# Kingfisher on the Bookshelf

Not my house, not sure whose, this a dream,
but I saw a flicker up there—No, *Kingfisher!*

Crested, iridescent, black-blue, hatpin eyes.
Last autumn in the gazebo I freed another.

This bird hunches among stacked books.
I reach up, cup my hands over the wings.

Should have considered those
needle claws, ice-pick beak.

At a door I release him, then worry: a nest
among all those books? Abandoned chicks?

"If you don't write for days, do
undone poems emerge as dreams?"

My kingfisher an omen?
Perhaps lone birds are.

Like feathers, should I gather dreams,
risk blood-letting beaks, open doors?

# Aftermath

After the black snake
slithers into the bluebird house,
swallows his prize, bursts out
the roof, wrecks the box,

he leaves on the lawn the nest
woven of moss, grass, down
plucked from the mother's breast,
and, glistening in the sun, his shed skin.

I have known men like this.

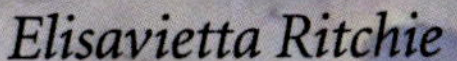

*Elisavietta Ritchie*

# Chickens Are Not Emotionally-Satisfying Pets

As I learned in a lone Malay hamlet,
final year of a marriage, fowl are not
loving, like cats, which he banned,

nor companionable, like the mutt
he got third-hand after I chased out
a midnight burglar while he slept.

Burnished auburn, emerald and gold,
the rooster strutted with audacity,
wattles wagged contempt for humankind.

The black hen might have felt
primordial compassion, for
day after day, no matter that

the door was to stay shut,
in she'd slip, rooster in pursuit,
stalk upstairs, leave her gift:

one beige egg, laid on my pillow
or in my bureau drawer
left open by mistake.

Were these fertilized?
Could I have incubated them,
turned foster mother to a flock?

But I recalled an adage,
Don't try to teach
your grandma to suck eggs,

found my darning needle, poked
a hole in the narrow end,
gulped the rich and slimy life inside.

# Dead-Hen Chronicles

Half the poets I know
have their barnyard tale
of shattered innocence:

a superannuated layer
plump enough
for the hatchet,

a rival rooster
strangled and plucked
for the Sunday pot.

Grandma's splattered apron.
My loss of faith
in the gap

between cunning beasts
from nursery tales
and dinner.

I was six, summering
on a farm beyond Chicago,
allowed to tend the hens.

Then my favorite red
scampered headless
around the yard

a feathered fountain—
Drenched,
I fled.

Age twelve, imbued
with scientific curiosity
in Pennsylvania,

I joined the older girls
in the plucking shed.
They'd done it before:

long narrow knife
up the throat,
stab the brain,

cut a certain nerve
to release the feathers.
At least these hens

were hung by the heels,
their blood flowed
in a bucket.

I learned to kill,
unfeather and gut
while we sang

"Gentille Allouette"
"My darlin' Clementine"
"Home on the Range"

I reached inside
my naked bird,
yanked out

gizzard, liver, heart,
limp spaghetti tubes—
"Don't pierce the bile!"

Might she still
harbor an egg?
My fingers groped

her hollows...
Suddenly she squawked—
I skipped that fricassee.

I've grown, tasted
most things once,
given up hoofed beasts.

Now Dr. Steinberg
urges chicken stew
for my anemia.

Onions, garlic,
celery, carrots,
bay leaves, sage—

Still, across the universe
that cry from inside
resounds, resounds.

## Ornithological Identification

*(After a visit to the Animal Preparation Laboratory,*
*Smithsonian Institution)*

I watched a crested merganser
lose his guts without flinching.
He didn't open his serrated beak to croak
when peeled back to the throat.
He was too stiff to care
hence was also unaware
I winced at the knife in his place,
the scalpel scraping his skull,
shuddered at the sawdust absorbing our blood
so the inside of our feathered skin could dry
enough for excelsior.

## On a Mid-Winter Gift of a Hummingbird Feeder

Corn tassels attract
hummingbirds en masse to fields
too soon stubbled, sere.

No corn here. Snowdrops
are brief, camellias complex
to unfold and probe.

Next spring hummingbirds
will find a pot of nectar
swinging from our oak.

## What Do You Do With a Dead Bird

Found beneath the water-oak: one wren
belly up. Wire legs, beak a black thorn,
splash of daffodil above the tail, a fan of gray.
Underside: three oblong patches, white.
Milkweed on his gold-striped breast.

He lies on my manuscripts tonight,
wings wide—to applaud, or to escape?
Pristine. Zapped in full song, full flight?

Can't toss a bird in the compost bin
with apple cores, orange rinds.
*Compose/Compost…*

Oh—darn, the door!
Clear up—What would visitors say
of a host who keeps dead birds?
*Weird taste for moribund things.*

Yet what no longer pecks or stings,
spears or talks, I'll hold and scrutinize.

Mortality's an expected guest.
Skulls are fine for saints to contemplate.
Permit this wingless sinner then
a cranium mere blueberry size.

## Preservation Problems

I know each summer here may be my last
so fling myself in cold October waves
beneath the flowing grebes and swans
and coots who refuge here and do not know
each summer here may be their last.

## Just Before Sunset

To catch the hour of gold in the cove
discard your coins of silver and tin,
platinum buckets, pails with holes,
the circular lens with the metal rim,
all bracelets, even the rings.

Walk out where beach and jetty end,
waves break in the last rays of sun,
jump over rocks and crabs,
step straight into wet and cold
mud-sand beneath the skin of sea.

Follow the black-and-white ducks.
They submerge and surface, dive again,
reappear, shake drops from their wings.
When at last you catch up, unsure where
you are, learn to swim before dark.

# In This Winged Instant

*1. July*
Dragonflies hover over the dock,
swallows dart from nests underneath,

gulls settle into a semi-circle
across the harbor mouth,

a spangled fritillary
perches on my palm,

a cormorant lands on a piling against
the red sun dappling a greying bay,

and already the first bats
scythe the wake of the rising moon,

there are indeed only yourself and myself
in an instant that will also take flight.

*2. December*
Fox prints and deer pock the snow
over the grass where we danced.

Our picnic table hosts banquets of snow.
Canvas chairs tip snow onto snow.

Skeletal weeds poke through crust.
The fig bush bears a snow harvest.

Beyond the sliver of beach, crabs
have shuffled deep in the channel,

fish fled under ice, or south. I don't
adjust to this change of season, still

long for summer, as for you, utterly.
Then a hundred swans avalanche to the cove.

Elisavietta Ritchie

## Two Cuckoos

Flushed from different glades
we fly on dangerous currents side by side
flight patterns intersect—

then we hide in stolen nests
of tangled thistles, twigs
and down from other breasts.

Yes, we're naughty birds,
predestined outsiders, thieves,
sloppy architects, must accept

cacophony of foreign neighborhoods,
estranged mates, be grateful for
whatever externals of respectability.

We would move to larger quarters,
find an osprey's nest with all the right
acoustics for our mirror melodies.

We'll be shot down for wandering off
course... Still we expand parabolas,
fly at higher altitudes,

drain the singing from each other's throats,
pierce the clouds,
and drown in ever wider skies.

## *Acknowledgments*

The author thanks the editors in whose publications the following poems appeared earlier, often in slightly different versions.

"Aftermath:" *Earth's Daughters,* Vol. #55, 2000; *The Spirit of the Walrus*, Bright Hill Press, NY, 2005; *Awaiting Permission to Land,* A Lyre Series Selection, (winner of the Anamnesis Manuscript Award), Cherry Grove Collections, WordTech Communications, Ohio, 2006, both © 2005 Elisavietta Ritchie;

"Chickens Are Not Emotionally Satisfying Pets:" *Oberon,* 2002; *The Spirit of the Walrus,* Bright Hill Press, 2005; *Awaiting Permission to Land*;

"Dead Hen Chronicles:" *The Ledge,* 1998, first prize, poetry; *The Spirit of the Walrus,* Bright Hill Press, 2005; *Awaiting Permission to Land*;

"Dialogue with Mourning Dove:" *The Broadkill Review*, Volume 3, Issue 6, 2009; *Cormorant Beyond the Compost;* Cherry Grove Series, WordTech Communications, © 2011 Elisavietta Ritchie;

"Dinner Partners:" *The Broadkill Review*, Volume 3, Issue 6, 2009; *Cormorant Beyond the Compost;*

"Epilogue:" excerpt from "Note for a Younger Self," *Blue Unicorn* for 2003; *Canadian Woman Studies* 2003; *Cormorant Beyond the Compost;*

"Feathers (or: Love on the Wing):" *The Broadkill Review*, Volume 3, Issue 6, 2009; *Cormorant Beyond the Compost;*

"Frontier Station:" *Poetry Now*, Volume 2, Number 4;

"Geese:" earlier version, *The Christian Science Monitor; Raking The Snow,* Washington Writers Publishing House, ©1982 Elisavietta Ritchie;

"In Flight:" *The Delaware Review,* 2008; *Cormorant Beyond the Compost;*

"In Search of Permanence:" *The Christian Science Monitor 1970; Tightening The Circle Over Eel Country,* Acropolis Books © 1974 Elisavietta Ritchie, Winner, Great Lakes Colleges Association's "New Writer's Award for Best First Book of Poetry 1975-76;

"Insomnia Cantatas:" *The Ledge* #29, 2005, their "poem of the month" September-October 2006; editor Timothy Monaghan nominated it for a 2007 Pushcart Prize; also published in *Confrontation*; *Awaiting Permission to Land*;

"In This Winged Instant:" *The Christian Science Monitor* ©1995; *Potomac Review,* 1996; *The Arc of the Storm,* Signal Books, © 1998 Elisavietta Ritchie;

"Just Before Sunset:"*Lalitamba* 2007; *The Light in Ordinary Things,* Fearless Books, 2009; *Cormorant Beyond the Compost;*

"John James Audubon: *Snowy Egret*:" earlier draft as "Beyond Newark New Jersey," *Concise,* 2009;

"Kingfisher on the Bookcase:"*Visions International,* #84, 2011; *From the Artist's Deathbed*; *Tiger Upstairs on Connecticut Avenue,* 2013;

"Odette Plies the Patuxent:" *The Broadkill Review,* Volume 3, Issue 6, 2009;

"Ornithological Identification:" *Yes,* circa 1970; *Tightening The Circle Over Eel Country*;

"Osprey:" *Ann Arbor Review* circa 2003;

"Presumptions:" *The Christian Science Monitor*, © August 22, 1996;

"Snowy Owl, Ontario:" *Little Patuxent Review*, 2009; *Cormorant Beyond the Compost*;

"Swan Story:" *Raking the Snow,* and in a journal first;

"Tarred Gull:" *Denver Post* circa 1967; *Tightening The Circle Over Eel Country;*

"Two-Cuckoo Poem:" *Moving To Larger Quarters,* Artists' and Writers' Collaborative, Manila, © 1977 Elisavietta Ritchie; *Cormorant Beyond the Compost;*

"Visitations: Omens:" *The Broadkill Review*, Volume 3, Issue 6, 2009.

"What Do You Do With a Dead Bird:" Visions International, 2008; *Cormorant Beyond the Compost;*

"Without the Mind, Nothing Exists:" *The Broadkill Review,* Volume 3, Issue 6, 2009; *Cormorant Beyond the Compost:*

"Yesterday's Owl:" *The Broadkill Review*, Volume 3, Issue 6, 2009; *Cormorant Beyond the Compost.*

*Elisavietta Ritchie's* work is widely published and anthologized. Individual stories, poems, creative non-fiction, photographs, and her translations from Russian, French, Macedonian and Indonesian have appeared in numerous publications in the United States and abroad, and her own work is translated into a dozen languages. Readings include the Library of Congress, Harbourfront, Folger Library, Pittsburgh International Forum, Harvard, and other universities, schools, and cultural centers in the United States and Canada, Australia, Russia, and, sponsored by the United States Information Agency, in Brazil, the Far East, and the Balkans.

Poet, writer, editor, and leader of workshops for adults and children, Ritchie attended the Sorbonne, Cornell University, and received a B.A. from University of California, Berkeley and an M.A. from American University in Washington, D.C. She served as president for poetry, then for fiction, for the Washington Writers' Publishing House, where she continues as a fiction editor.

Composers Jackson Berkey, David Owens, David L. Brunner, and others, have transformed her poems for voice and piano. Artist-historian Donald Shomette superimposed her poems on a portfolio of his photographs.

*Megan Richard* comes from a long line of creative women, her mother, grandmother, and great-grandmother were all talented artists. Megan finds inspiration for her artwork from the natural world. Influences come from living by the Chesapeake Bay and Patuxent River, hiking in the Cascades and Adirondacks and long summers spent with her family on Manitoulin Island in Lake Huron.

Megan practices art in watercolor, fluid acrylics, inks and casein, also adding elements of collage and printing to her work, discovering new techniques to create works with interesting textures and colors.

Megan has a B.A. in Fine Arts from Ohio Wesleyan University. She has studied watercolor painting with artist Mary Blumberg at the Studio School at Annmarie Sculpture Garden in Dowell, Maryland and has taken classes at the Art League School in Alexandria, Virginia. Megan gives private art lessons to children. She also teaches children's art classes at Annmarie Garden in Calvert County, Maryland, and at the Bowie Montessori Children's House encouraging the creative endeavors of her students.

*"Good morning little birdies,
good morning to you.
I love my little birdies
and they love me too."*

My mother, Jocelyn Tillman, was a lover of art, poetry and birds. She sang this little song each morning to her beloved little finches perched next to our kitchen sink and to the many songbirds visiting our feeders during the winter. With great love and admiration, I dedicate these paintings to her memory and to the memory of the little feathered friends she loved so much.

Megan Richard